Our
Washington

George and Rhonda Ostertag

Voyageur Press

First published in 2008 by Voyageur Press, an imprint of MBI Publishing Company LLC, 400 First Avenue North, Suite 300, Minneapolis, MN 55401 USA

The information in this book is true and complete to the best of our knowledge. All recommendations are made without any guarantee on the part of the author or Publisher, who also disclaim any liability incurred in connection with the use of this data or specific details. We recognize, further, that some words, model names, and designations mentioned herein are the property of the trademark holder. We use them for identification purposes only. This is not an official publication.

Voyageur Press titles are also available at discounts in bulk quantity for industrial or sales-promotional use. For details write to Special Sales Manager at MBI Publishing Company, 400 First Avenue North, Suite 300, Minneapolis, MN 55401 USA.

To find out more about our books, join us online at www.voyageurpress.com.

Library of Congress Cataloging-in-Publication Data

Ostertag, George, 1957 –
  Our Washington / George and Rhonda Ostertag.
    p. cm.
  ISBN 978-0-7603-2920-7 1. Washington (State)—Pictorial works. 2. Landscape—Washington (State)—Pictorial works. 3. Natural history—Washington (State)—Pictorial works. I. Ostertag, Rhonda, 1957- II. Title.
  F892.O88 2008
  917.970022'2—dc22
                              2007046259

Editor: Josh Leventhal
Designer: Danielle Smith

Printed in Hong Kong

ON THE FRONT COVER
Abbey Island from Ruby Beach, Olympic National Park.

ON THE BACK COVER
Top: Waterfall on Big Spring Creek, Gifford Pinchot National Forest.
Bottom Left: Sunrise glow on Mount Rainier in autumn.
Bottom Right: Abandoned homestead with balsamroot at Methow Wildlife Area.

PAGE 1
Cape Flattery Trail on the Makah Indian Reservation leads to the extreme northwestern tip of the Olympic Peninsula, the farthest northwest point in the lower forty-eight states, offering dramatic views of the Cape Flattery shoreline.

PAGE 2
Mukilteo Light has guided mariners navigating the waters of Puget Sound since 1906. The light's octagonal wooden tower rises thirty feet. The classic lighthouse was designed by C. W. Leick.

PAGE 3
Built for the 1962 World's Fair, the Space Needle in Seattle was the tallest building west of the Mississippi at the time. The observation deck is 520 feet above the ground, and the halo measures 138 feet in diameter.

PAGE 4
Mount Adams is one in the chain of Cascade volcanoes stretching from Mount Garibaldi in British Columbia to Mount Lassen in Northern California. It is seen here from Goat Ridge in Goat Rocks Wilderness, Mount Baker–Snoqualmie National Forest.

PAGE 5, TOP
Towering Douglas firs interspersed with western red cedar and western hemlock shape the ancient woodland at Lewis and Clark State Park, south of Chehalis.

PAGE 5, BOTTOM
Abandoned ranch houses, such as this one in the Methow Wildlife Area near Winthrop, recall early efforts to eke out an existence on the harsh Washington frontier.

ON THE TITLE PAGE
Sunrise Point in Mount Rainier National Park serves up this image of Mount Adams. While most visitors lock eyes on Mount Rainier during the sunrise, over-the-shoulder views reveal Mount Adams.

ON THE TITLE PAGE, INSET
Cascades, waterfalls, and mosses punctuate Big Spring Creek and many waterways threading through Gifford Pinchot National Forest.

The romance of the sea is incomplete without the majesty of the tall ships. Today, tour companies operate tall-ship excursions, training camps, and boat tours, and these mirrors to the past gather at festivals all along the western coast. The sails of this lady were spied in Shark Reef Sanctuary off Lopez Island.

At Lime Kiln Point State Park, on the west side of San Juan Island, the sun sets on the 1919 Lime Kiln Lighthouse. The park and the light take their names from the lime kilns that were built at the site in 1860. Today, the lighthouse building doubles as an orca whale research site. Lime Kiln Point is perhaps the best land based whale-viewing site on Puget Sound.

Orca whales travel just offshore from Lime Kiln Point State Park. Whale-watching season runs from May through September, with peak sightings in June and July. Besides orcas, keen-eyed visitors can spy Minke whales, porpoises, sea lions, seals, and otters.

Today, Roche Harbor is noted for its crisp white buildings, tranquil gardens, tourist shops, and bustling marina, but it began as a company town in 1886, founded by and kept under the thumb of John S. McMillin. McMillin owned the Roche Harbor Lime and Cement Company, billed as the largest lime works west of the Mississippi. Workers were paid in company scrip redeemable only at the McMillin-owned company store.

Due to unclear wording in the border treaty of 1846, the English and the Americans squared off over San Juan Island, each maintaining a camp to protect its country's interests. All remained relatively quiet until a dispute over a dead pig nearly brought the countries to war in 1859. Depicted here is the blockhouse and formal garden at the English Camp, now part of San Juan Island National Historical Park.

BELOW

The waters, eagles, and sea life around the San Juan Islands attract many sea kayaking enthusiasts to the area. These kayaks were put into shore at Deer Harbor on Orcas Island.

ABOVE

With one foot in Canada and the other in the United States, the sixty-seven-foot-tall International Peace Arch straddles the border between Douglas, British Columbia, and Blaine, Washington. Built in 1921, the arch was the first monument ever erected in honor of world peace. The centennial of the Treaty of Ghent (which ended the War of 1812) prompted its construction.

RIGHT

Hovander Homestead County Park in Ferndale includes this 1911 barn, one of the largest wooden barns in Whatcom County, standing sixty feet tall. The barn and the 1903 mansion were built by Hokan Hovander, a Swedish architect who settled here. Farm animals, flower gardens, a pumpkin patch, and antique farm equipment keep the site's history alive. The adjacent 720-acre Tennant Lake Wildlife Area keeps the area natural and expands exploration.

LEFT

Near the Canadian border in Whatcom County, Lynden extends a Dutch welcome with its seventy-two-foot working windmill. The tidy, picturesque village furthers the spell with its classic Dutch-gabled architecture along Front Street, a whimsical 142-foot-long Holland-themed mural, and a Holland Days celebration in May, featuring a traditional street sweeping and "klompen" dancers.

BELOW

Each spring a colorful palette of tulips attracts thousands of people to the country roads of Skagit County. The region is one of the nation's major producers of tulip, daffodil, and iris bulbs. Barns, the distant Olympics, Mount Baker, and tractors complement the color scheme. Field rotations to protect the health of the bulbs can change the canvas from year to year.

OPPOSITE

Bellingham's Big Rock Garden Park occupies a woodland setting above Lake Whatcom. Besides blooms and trees, the garden encompasses an eclectic collection of art and sculpture, including the *Sun Mask*, by Jimmy Joseph, honoring Native Americans. The art is revealed in surprising ways along twisting garden paths.

In Whatcom Falls County Park, in Bellingham, moss, ferns, rhododendron, and draping maples complement this picturesque stone bridge built by the Works Progress Administration (WPA) in 1939. Roosevelt's WPA employed great numbers of Depression-era workers in projects that benefitted the nation: roads, parks, public buildings, and cultural advancements.

Mount Erie, the heart of Mount Erie Park, rises nearly 1,300 feet above Anacortes and draws visitors skyward with stunning San Juan Islands overlooks, clear-day views of the Olympics and Mounts Baker and Rainier, and close-up looks at the surrounding countryside. This view spans Lake Campbell toward Skagit Bay.

LEFT

Built in 1861 and rebuilt in 1903, Whidbey Island's Admiralty Head Light guided Puget Sound mariners along the island until 1922, when its light was extinguished. The light now sits within the borders of Fort Casey State Park in Ebey's Landing National Historic Reserve, attracting tourists, photographers, and wedding parties. The romance of a lighthouse never dims.

LEFT

The Washington State Ferry system is both a transportation jewel and a Washington trademark. The system efficiently serves commuters and treats tourists to scenic travel. Eagles, whales, and porpoises; pleasure boats and working ships; and islands and cityscapes engage passengers on the Puget Sound waters. This ferry was photographed from Mukilteo Lighthouse Park in Mukilteo.

At Olympic Beach in Edmonds, the lights from the fishing pier dance on the waters, as fishermen continue to cast into the night. The 950-foot-long public pier never closes. Anglers cast for salmon and bottom fish and jig for squid. The Edmonds waterfront was the traditional fishing grounds of the Snohomish tribe, and it once boasted the largest charter fishing fleet on Puget Sound. It continues to be an important port city and ferry landing.

ABOVE

Low tides on Hood Canal in Twanoh State Park say, "Grab your buckets, it's time to tidepool." Hood Canal is noted for its plentiful seafood. All ages are attracted by the mystery and rich life of this ocean-influenced natural canal.

RIGHT

Oyster harvesting is a popular Washington pastime. Gloves, a sturdy sharp tool or knife to pry open the oyster shells, and a dose of persistence are needed to liberate the succulent prizes. Cold, oxygen-rich water with a suitable salinity produces plump, juicy oysters. The rich tidal beds at Duckabush Wildlife Area busied this oyster shucker.

The story of Bremerton cannot be told without mention of the U.S. Navy. It is a tie that traces back to 1891, when William Bremer convinced the U.S. Navy to construct a naval shipyard here. The USS *Turner Joy,* docked at the Bremerton Boardwalk, has become an emblem of the city. The destroyer, now a navy memorial, had a distinguished naval career before being retired and becoming a permanent Bremerton attraction.

ABOVE

This popular landmark at Fort Worden State Park is known as "Alexander's Castle." It has a decided Scottish-castle architecture. It was built in 1883, near Point Wilson, by the Reverend John Alexander as a gift for his intended Scottish bride. But when he returned to his homeland to retrieve her, she had married another. He occupied the castle alone, and later the military at Fort Worden put the building to various uses.

The distant snowy crest of the Olympic Mountains overlooks the Boat Haven moorage at Port Townsend. Pleasure crafts, working fishing boats, and other commercial vessels share the moorage. Port Townsend is home to the acclaimed Wooden Boat Foundation and the Northwest School of Wooden Boat Building.

OPPOSITE

Tiny Port Gamble enchants with New England–style homes along maple-lined streets. This sawmill company town was designed to reflect the hometown of the city founders: East Machias, Maine. Today, the mill is closed, but the town is a National Historic Landmark. Seen here is the elaborate home of the resident mill manager, the 1888 William Walker–Edwin Ames House.

Gas Works Park at the north end of Lake Union affords a perfect vantage point from which to take in downtown Seattle and the boating on Lake Union. Lake Union was landlocked until the Lake Washington Ship Canal was constructed to link Lake Washington to Puget Sound. The attractive Seattle skyline makes Lake Union popular for tour boats and all manner of leisure craft: kayaks, sculls, sailboats, and even traditional Indian canoes.

One of the world's first skyscrapers, the Smith Tower (built 1910–1914) dominates the skyline with its shining white facade, many windows, and pyramid top. The seasonal flower baskets adorning the city's streets fashion the perfect frame for this downtown landmark. The tower's thirty-fifth-floor observation deck turns attention back on the city.

On the main campus of the University of Washington, in Seattle, the Henry Suzzallo Memorial Library (named for a former University president) has a commanding presence. Its bold Tudor-Gothic collegiate architecture was designed in 1923 by Carl Gould, a prominent Seattle architect and a founder of the University of Washington Architecture Department.

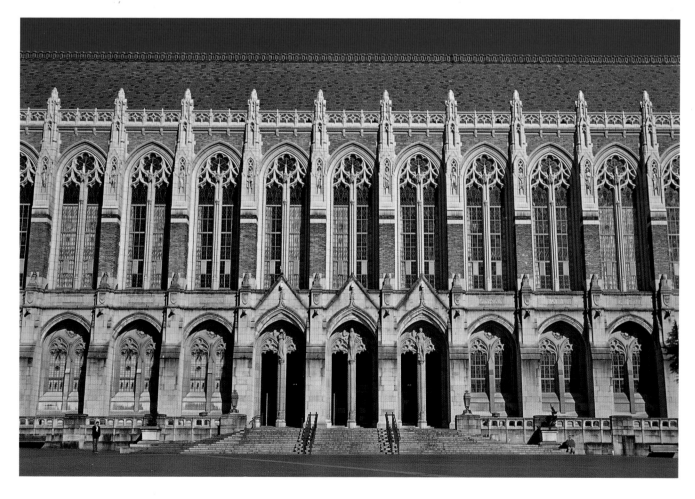

OPPOSITE

Kerry Park on Queen Anne Hill attracts photographers with stunning late-day and nighttime shots of Seattle. The park was a gift to the city in 1927 from Mr. and Mrs. Albert Sperry Kerry Sr. so all could enjoy the view. The night-lit Space Needle rightfully claims center stage at Seattle Center; on clear days, Mount Rainier joins the vista.

ABOVE

The colorful history of Seattle's Pioneer Square Tlingit totem pole begins with its questionable "liberation" by city leaders from its traditional Alaskan location. Carved of hemlock, the original sixty-foot pole dated back to 1790 and graced the square from October 1899 until 1938, when it fell victim to an arsonist. The pole's remains were sent to Tlingit artisans in Ketchikan, Alaska, for replication. Like the original, the present cedar pole represents the Raven Clan.

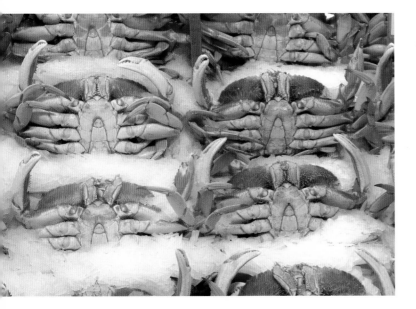

LEFT

A true Seattle icon, the Pike Place Public Market springs to life long before the shopkeepers entertain shoppers and tourists. Wheelbarrows of crushed ice and pounds of fresh fish, clams, crab, shrimp, and lobster are meticulously displayed for the day's business. Cut flowers fresh from the field are arranged in bountiful bouquets, colorful aprons fly from the rafters, and baked goods scent the air.

ABOVE

Pike Place Public Market began in 1907 and has survived numerous attempts to bring about its demise in the name of modernization. The market's street-level stalls and subterranean shops provide a lively venue where farmers, fishers, flower growers, bakers, artisans, and performers reach buyers face-to-face, drawing locals and tourists alike.

Seattle's Japanese-American Kubota Garden, a twenty-acre public garden, shapes a tranquil hill-and-valley escape with springs, streams, ponds, waterfalls, leaves, trees, blooms, and stones. The sixty-year vision of Fujitaro Kubota, a self-taught gardener, this Eden successfully blends native Northwest vegetation with Japanese influences from its marriages of plants and water to the paths, gates, sculptures, and classic red Moon Bridge.

The 1894 Aaron Neely House near Auburn, dressed here in fourth of July celebration, is a King County landmark. The Classical Revival farmhouse overlooks the land the Neely family cultivated in the Green River Valley, but modern forces have since rewritten the valley tapestry. The home was an important social center in its day. Today, it serves as a museum.

Downtown Tacoma, a bustling transportation hub, has experienced a cultural Renaissance in recent decades. A thriving arts and social offering of theaters, clubs, shops, eateries, and museums has brought a renewed interest in and vibrancy to the city core.

ABOVE

The ultramodern 21st Street suspension bridge joins Tacoma's other city landmarks: Union Station, the shining stainless-steel Museum of Glass, the Chihuly Bridge of Glass, and the Tacoma Dome.

LEFT

This is the clock tower of Old City Hall, the original Italian Renaissance–style City Hall that rose above the streets of Tacoma in 1893. The stately building designed by E. A. Hatherton of San Francisco was a symbol of civic pride and represented optimism in the city's future. An economic crash that same year temporarily dimmed that optimism, but the building continues to be a source of civic pride.

LEFT

Artist Larry Anderson's *New Beginnings* stands at the entry to Tacoma's renovated historic Union Station. The bronze statue depicts an arriving train passenger ready to seize prosperity.

RIGHT

In March 1994, Tacoma's Union Station became the venue for "Chihuly at Union Station," featuring the glass creations of locally grown but world-renowned artist Dale Chihuly. Seen here beneath the great dome is the *End of the Day* chandelier. Chihuly has gained fame for his revolutionary and complex large-scale, team-produced contemporary glass sculptures. The artist traces his monumental-scale work to this hometown project at Union Station.

LEGISLATIVE · BUILDING

OPPOSITE

The Legislative Building of the Washington State Capitol in Olympia took six years to build and was completed in 1928. It was designed by New York architects Wilder and White, who won the 1911 design competition for the project. The building has withstood three earthquakes and some heated political debate.

ABOVE

On the West Campus of the Capitol, just northeast of the Legislative Building, *Winged Victory* is the 1938 bronze memorial honoring the veterans of World War I. Created by Alonzo Victor Lewis, the memorial features the goddess Nike extending an olive branch above four figures: a soldier, sailor, marine, and Red Cross nurse. It is seen here under the nighttime spotlight.

ABOVE

Tivoli Fountain, given to the state by the Olympia-Tumwater Foundation, is another attraction on the Capitol's West Campus. Composed of metal and stone, this fountain is modeled after a village fountain in Tivoli, Italy. It was a version of this fountain in Copenhagen, Denmark, however, that inspired foundation president Peter Schmidt to duplicate it in Washington.

The Bluff Trail at Dungeness National Wildlife Refuge serves up this sunset cliff view looking out to the Strait of Juan de Fuca. The 631-acre refuge is located near Sequim in Clallam County.

A fishing boat moves through the waters off Cape Flattery, at the northwestern tip of the Olympic Peninsula. Cape Flattery sits just northwest of the Makah Indian fishing village of Neah Bay. Commercial fishing remains a mainstay of the Makah people. The name "Makah," given to the tribe by their neighbors, means "generous with food."

On the Quileute Indian Reservation, boat masts partition this La Push Harbor view. The harbor is home to the tribe's small fishing and crabbing fleet. The culture and livelihood of the Quileute people have always been tied to the sea. The Quileute were expert fishers, sealers, and whalers. Today, the tribe fishes and processes and markets salmon at their small seafood plant.

LEFT

Accessed only by hiking trail, on the beach between Cape Alava and Sand Point in Olympic National Park, more than forty primitive petroglyphs decorate the coastal rocks in the vicinity of Wedding Rock. Carved into the rock are images of orcas, Indian masks, ovals, ships, hunters, and fishers. The artists likely were inhabitants of the Ozette Indian village at Cape Alava that was buried in a mudslide 500 years ago.

ABOVE

The sun peacefully sets over Destruction Island and Lighthouse, about three miles offshore from Olympic National Park. The thirty-acre tabletop island is bordered by steep bluffs. Early Spanish and British explorers were massacred while visiting the island and nearby coast, hence the island's ominous name.

OPPOSITE

The wet sand of low tide reflects Abbey Island at Ruby Beach in Olympic National Park. Abbey Island reportedly received its name in the 1866 U.S. Coast Survey for its resemblance to an ancient abbey. Ruby Beach is named for the tiny grains of red garnet in its sand.

Historic Lake Quinault Lodge, built in 1926, is nestled in a temperate-zone rainforest above Lake Quinault in Olympic National Forest. On the National Register of Historic Places, this rustic hotel, with its steep roof, towering fireplace, and blue-shuttered windows, seamlessly blends into its natural setting. President Franklin D. Roosevelt stayed here in 1937, on a visit that prompted his signing the bill to create Olympic National Park.

Olympic National Park is one of the nation's most diverse parks, composed of a temperate rainforest, a wilderness coast, and the high-peak grandeur of the Olympic Mountains. Enveloped in greenery, Marymere Falls in the Barnes Creek drainage spills ninety feet in an old-growth setting near Lake Crescent.

The deeply incised, steep-sided peaks of the Olympic Mountains are not especially tall (Mount Olympus is less than 8,000 feet high), but the western slopes of these mountains receive more precipitation than anywhere else in the lower forty-eight states. From December to March, the mountains' precipitation occurs as snow, transforming the Olympics into a wonderland, as seen here from Hurricane Ridge.

A mountain goat strides through a wildflower meadow near Mount Angeles in Olympic National Park. Although you cannot see it, controversy surrounds the goat. The park service maintains that mountain goats are nonnative to the Olympic Mountains, introduced here in the 1920s, and therefore should go. Other parties point to recorded goat sightings before the 1920s and urge the animals be kept.

Winter's icy brine transforms this forest on Hurricane Ridge into a peculiar gallery of living sculpture. The park service maintains Hurricane Ridge (elevation 5,240 feet) for winter recreation; it is reached by a winding seventeen-mile road. A small downhill ski area, snow play area, cross-country ski trails, and snowshoeing engage Hurricane Ridge visitors.

Spring migratory shorebirds congregate on Willapa Bay, in Willapa National Wildlife Refuge. The small birds stop over to feed on the nutrient-rich estuary flats, refueling for the long journey north to their summer habitats.

This quiet meeting of land and sea is at Damon Point State Park on the Ocean Shores Peninsula. Damon Point is a mile-long, half-mile-wide jut formed by accretion (the opposite action of erosion, where sands accumulate). The beach is wild enough to support nesting snowy plovers.

ABOVE

This old fishing building on Willapa Bay is located in the village of Nahcotta, on the Long Beach Peninsula. Nahcotta, a fishing port and oyster harvesting and shipping community, takes its name from the Chinook Indian leader, Chief Nahcati, whose camp was near here.

LEFT

This crab ring of Dungeness crab awaits sorting on the fishing pier at Nahcotta's Port of Peninsula. The Long Beach area is known for its recreational fishing, crabbing, and shellfish harvesting, as well as its commercial fishing.

In Long Beach, this elevated dune boardwalk parallels the beach for a half mile, providing coastal overlooks and accessing the Discovery Trail, which commemorates Lewis and Clark. In 1805, William Clark journeyed from present-day Ilwaco to what is now Long Beach.

A beach gateway arch announces Long Beach's claim to fame: the "World's Longest Beach." Long Beach Peninsula rolls out twenty-nine miles of unbroken ocean beach for fun in the sun, including beach driving. Kite flying, surf fishing, and sunset gazing are more traditional pursuits.

Bright strings of kites color the skies at the Ocean Shores Sand and Sawdust Festival. Reliable winds on the Long Beach Peninsula are ideal for kite flying. Several festivals dedicated to kites take place throughout the year, attracting international competitors. The town of Long Beach is home to the World Kite Museum.

RIGHT

Art, architecture, and sand collide in magical ways at the Sandcastle Contest at the Ocean Shores Sand and Sawdust Festival. Buckets of water, shovels, trowels, and brushes coax the art from the sand.

Old buoys and a simple "TUNA" sign beckon buyers to a shop selling fresh fish in Ilwaco. Commercial fishing brings in tuna, salmon, halibut and other bottom fish, crab, and shrimp. Ilwaco sportfishers fish West Coast and Alaskan waters.

An early-morning fog wraps the fishing boats moored at Ilwaco harbor in a chilly aura of mystery. Since the days of the Chinook Indians, this has been an important fishing village.

North Head Lighthouse (1896) was the second light constructed at Cape Disappointment to guide mariners around the treacherous Columbia River Bar. The first was the Cape Disappointment Light, built in 1856. The North Head beacon illuminates the way for vessels arriving from the north, which before 1896 had been left in the dark. Between 1725 and 1961, the Columbia River Bar claimed more than 200 ships.

The sun sets on tiny cliff-lined Dead Man's Cove at Cape Disappointment State Park, part of Lewis and Clark National Historical Park. Although beautiful, the Cape Disappointment coastline has a history of deadly shipwrecks, necessitating the building of two lighthouses.

On Chinook Point, Fort Columbia State Park (now part of Lewis and Clark National Historical Park) preserves the military fort that protected the Columbia River between 1896 and 1947. Twelve historic wood-frame buildings remain from the military complex.

LEFT

The town of Winlock gained recognition for its hatcheries that produced 2.5 million chicks annually. So, an egg—the Winlock Egg—was the natural choice to represent the town. The original idea for the egg was hatched in 1920, and the egg was constructed of concrete. The current fiberglass version, made by Beverly Roberts in 1990, is the fourth egg.

LEFT

West of Chehalis in Claquato, the pioneer Claquato Church is the oldest church in Washington still in use at its original site. The church dates back to 1858 and is notable for its crown of thorns steeple.

North of Castle Rock, the Laughlin Round Barn is one of the last surviving round barns in Washington. In 1986, it was added to the National Register of Historic Places. Samuel Davidson Laughlin modeled his round barn after ones he'd admired in Oregon. After a windstorm packing seventy-five-mile-per-hour winds toppled the original structure in 1995, the barn was restored.

This attractive wooden bridge, donated to the city of Longview by the Weyerhaeuser Company in celebration of the company's centennial, leads to the Japanese Garden on an island within Lake Sacajawea Park. It is a second incarnation for the island, which first held a garden in 1924. That garden was abandoned when the original bridge deteriorated and had to be removed. The current bridge symbolizes the sister-city relationship between Longview and Waco, Japan.

The still-operational 1876 Cedar Creek Grist Mill, east of Woodland, is a National Historic Site and a working museum. The water-powered mill was built by George Woodham and sons and served the farm families of Clark County, grinding grain for flour and animal feed. Besides fulfilling its traditional role, the mill doubled as a social center, hosting dances and meetings.

This is the stockade at Fort Vancouver National Historic Site in Vancouver National Historic Reserve. This historic fort was a center of commerce and trade, as well as a defensive post, built by the London-based Hudson's Bay Company in 1825 to ensure its position in the region and serve its Columbia fur operation. The fort later assisted arriving Oregon Trail pioneers, helping them resupply for settlement.

This is the Grant House on Officers' Row in Vancouver National Historic Reserve. Ulysses S. Grant, Civil War general and U.S. president, was stationed at the Vancouver Barracks in the 1850s. Although this commanding general's quarters bears his name, Grant never lived here, but he did work here. Today, the Grant House holds a restaurant.

The hiss of fire and the ringing of hammered iron continue to sound at the blacksmith shop at Fort Vancouver National Historic Site. In the frontier, the blacksmith was pivotal to a community, producing various parts, tools, traps, nails, and items for trade with the Indians. Fort Vancouver's blacksmith shop, the largest in Oregon Country, employed four full-time smiths and several helpers.

This bronze salmon sculpture is an integral part of the Salmon Run Bell Tower in Vancouver's Esther Short Park, the oldest public square in the state. The sixty-nine-foot-tall bell tower attracts an audience with its bell ringing and animated glockenspiel scenes portraying a Chinook Indian legend.

ABOVE

The Columbia River is a vital waterway, active with barge, sternwheeler, and fishing boat traffic and the bouncing rides of sailboarders. The mighty river flows 1,200 miles from its origins at the base of the Canadian Rockies to the Pacific Ocean. Where the river cut a course through the Cascade Mountains, the Columbia River Gorge stretches for 100 miles between 3,000-foot cliffs.

The Columbia River Gorge National Scenic Area, established in 1986, encompasses the Oregon and Washington shores of this great river. Washington's State Route 14 travels the north side of the Columbia River Gorge, rounding up spectacular views, such as this one from Cape Horn, as well as a wealth of trails, waterfalls, cliff promontories, and historic sites.

ABOVE

Chamberlain Lake Viewpoint provides this sunrise view of the Columbia River Gorge. Such a peaceful scene provides little clue that 17,000 years ago, a sequence of gargantuan Ice Age floods known as the Missoula Floods deluged the Columbia River with water, rock, and debris, gouging out this dramatic cleft between Washington and Oregon.

OPPOSITE

A decorated Christmas tree in the window and holiday lights add to the warm welcome of Skamania Lodge on a winter's night. Although modern, with its uses of stone, heavy timbers, and Native American art, the charm of this lodge in the Columbia River Gorge resonates back to the traditional lodges of the early twentieth century.

Mosses cling to the zigzagging rustic wooden fence at the viewpoint for Lower Lewis River Falls in Gifford Pinchot National Forest. A trio of waterfalls punctuates the Upper Lewis River, but the setting of low-elevation old-growth forest is just as much a part of the river's invitation.

Tucked in a dark mossy hollow on Big Spring Creek in Gifford Pinchot National Forest, this picturesque waterfall is easily missed along Forest Road 23. But once found, it is not soon forgotten. It captivates not with height nor with volume, but with charm.

ABOVE

The thirty-five-foot-tall Lower Lewis River Falls graces a fractured cliff and spans the width of the Upper Lewis River in Gifford Pinchot National Forest. Upstream, a middle and an upper falls similarly enliven the river.

Mount Adams, standing 12,276 feet tall and graced by a dozen glaciers, looms above a barn on Camas Prairie in Klickitat County. The second-tallest peak in Washington (after Mount Rainier), Adams figures prominently in Yakama culture, and the mountain's huckleberry fields are widely cherished; many are set aside for Indian-use only. The eastern half of the mountain sits within the Yakama Indian Reservation.

Johnston Ridge provides this grand view of the blown-out crater on the north face of Mount St. Helens. The ridge carries the name of the dedicated U.S. Geological Survey volcanologist who lost his life here on May 18, 1980, monitoring the mountain's activity. He was one of fifty-seven people who died in the eruption. The vantage sits within five miles of the restless crater, offering the closest drive-to view of the mountain.

At Mount St. Helens National Volcanic Monument, mats of logs stripped naked of bark in the 1980 eruption still float like algae on the surface of Spirit Lake. Many others have sunk to the bottom. Spirit Lake lay in the direct path of the gigantic landslide of the eruption. Today, the lake bottom sits 100 feet higher than the historic lake surface.

RIGHT

In just three minutes' time, the eruptive belch of Mount St. Helens seared and flattened 230 square miles of ancient forest in a fan around the north side of the mountain. Even as the new forest grows, these ghostly snags stand in testament of the cataclysmic event.

The Mount St. Helens view through the windows at the Johnston Ridge Observatory holds an onlooker spellbound. This day the atmospheric disturbance was only fog. The observatory is named for volcanologist David A. Johnston. While taking measurements here on May 18, 1980, he radioed in: "Vancouver, Vancouver, this is it!" before being overtaken.

This yellow-brick road of Pierce County daffodils leads the eye to Mount Rainier's regal presence. With a summit elevation of 14,410 feet, Mount Rainier commands the stage for miles in all directions. Even Oregonians share in the view.

ABOVE

This is Mount Rainier as seen from Paradise in Mount Rainier National Park. Autumn's palette of red and gold claims Paradise Meadows, but snow is not far off. The National Park Service bills Paradise (elevation 5,400 feet) as the snowiest place on earth where snow records are kept. In the winter of 1971–1972, Paradise set a world record with a whopping 1,122 inches of snow.

LEFT

The tops of young firs pierce through the autumn-colored thicket of blueberry bushes and spirea shrubs at Paradise Meadows. A network of paths explore the meadows. Black bears attracted by the berries can sometimes be seen.

In wintertime, Mount Rainier seduces with pristine snow and quiet, wonderland settings. Snow typically arrives in late October, transforming landscapes.

LEFT

Despite their fragile appearance, glacier lilies are among the first wildflowers to usher in springtime at Mount Rainier National Park. Historically, Native Americans harvested the corms (the bulblike bases) of these plants for food.

OPPOSITE

In Mount Rainier National Park, cascades thread over and through rocks while racing away from Spray Falls, a popular hiking destination. The misting falls slips more than 300 feet down a bulbous cliff.

RIGHT

The elegant black-crested, dark blue Steller's jay with the chastising call commonly adorns the conifer branches in Mount Rainier National Park, but especially when the branches provide a good view of a picnic lunch. Steller's jays feed on insects, seeds, nuts, berries, and other birds' eggs. They will hoard food in territorial caches, for times when food is less plentiful.

LEFT

The pika—a tiny, round cousin of the rabbit—lives in rocky mountain environments and communicates with high-pitched alarm shrieks. This one dwells in Mount Rainier National Park. The pika does not hibernate in winter, so it must gather and dry grasses and other vegetation before the snow comes.

OPPOSITE

At the 5,600-foot elevation in Mount Rainier National Park, lupines paint Grand Park's two-mile-long meadow in splashes of purple. Reached by backcountry trail, this lofty mesa northeast of the mountain is alternately characterized by grand views and atmospheric moodiness.

The thunderous, 270-foot leap of Snoqualmie Falls in the town of Snoqualmie attracts more than 1.5 million visitors annually. Trails and observation decks present the waterfall and its enfolding canyon. A small powerhouse and picturesque Salish Lodge overlook the head of the falls. In 1889, when the first passenger train arrived in town, Charles Blondin (the French acrobat famous for a Niagara Falls tightrope walk) successfully walked a tightrope across this waterfall canyon.

BELOW

The summit of Mount Pilchuck provided this greeting to a new day. In Mount Pilchuck State Park, the namesake peak lifts visitors 5,324 feet above sea level and extends views toward the Cascades, the Olympics, and the Puget Sound. The old fire lookout atop the mountain hasn't been staffed since the 1960s.

At the 5,000-foot elevation in the Alpine Lakes Wilderness of Wenatchee National Forest, Lake Stuart sits in a picturesque cirque cupped by Jack Ridge (seen here) and impressive Mount Stuart. Although discovery of the Alpine Lakes region was delayed, the calls for its preservation came early. In the 1930s the area was proposed for Ice Peaks National Park.

ABOVE

Red Top Lookout in Wenatchee National Forest south of the Stuart Range enjoys an inspired clifftop location. The lookout was added to the National Historic Lookout Register in 1997. The summit offers panoramic viewing of the Stuart Range and the Cascade volcanoes and is an excellent hawk-watch post. For years, the slopes of Red Top have attracted rockhounds searching for 350-million-year-old jasper geodes.

Bundled-up rafters take on the Skagit River during the winter bald eagle watch. Several hundred of the regal birds spend their winter in the Skagit River Bald Eagle Natural Area. Their arrival coincides with the spawning runs of chum salmon. The eagles start appearing in November, with numbers dwindling by mid-March. Mid-January into February is peak time for eagle watching.

Washington's Skagit Valley is the preferred wintering site chosen by the snow geese, with tens of thousands taking to the fields. Here, a mass liftoff at Skagit Wildlife Area overtakes the Mount Baker view. This wildlife area along the Pacific Flyway also hosts tundra and trumpeter swans and migrating shorebirds.

The dynamic liquid duo of Watson Lakes puts a blue shimmer on the 14,000-acre Noisy-Diobsud Wilderness in Mount Baker–Snoqualmie National Forest. The wilderness area is named for the Noisy Creek draining north and the Diobsud Creek draining south.

Mount Baker Scenic Byway carries hundreds of photographers each year to the shores of Picture Lake for this classic shot of Mount Shuksan and its watery double. The low light of late day finds photographers shoulder-to-shoulder poised for the shot.

LEFT

Franklin Falls in Mount Baker–Snoqualmie National Forest is one of several waterfalls on the South Fork Snoqualmie River. The overall drop of Franklin Falls measures 135 feet and spills in three stages; shown here is the lower, 70-foot stage. Front-row viewing is first-rate, if you don't mind getting wet.

BELOW

Winter snow piles up on the Great Northern Railway caboose at the Iron Goat Interpretive Site. This site provides access to the Iron Goat Trail along the Stevens Pass Greenway, a scenic byway. Making use of abandoned sections of the Great Northern Railway, the Iron Goat recreational trail is an example of the rails-to-trails movement sweeping the nation.

Johannesburg Mountain in North Cascades National Park looms large above the Cascade Pass Trailhead. The mountain is marked by its hanging glaciers, tinsel melt waters, and jagged-rock skyline. The North Cascades National Park Service Complex features more glaciers than anywhere else in the lower forty-eight states.

In Okanogan National Forest, the cool temperatures of fall turn the needles of the western larches around Cutthroat Lake to gold. The western larch is a mountain native that grows in Montana, Idaho, Oregon, Washington, and British Columbia. Unlike other conifers, it is deciduous.

Washington Pass Scenic Overlook in the Okanogan National Forest affords this view of the massive granite dome known as Liberty Bell in the North Cascades. Liberty Bell Mountain has a summit elevation of 7,720 feet and a striking vertical relief.

ABOVE

Cattail-rimmed, twenty-four-acre Forde Lake in Sinlahekin Wildlife Area is ideal for a rowboat and a fishing pole. Sinlahekin Wildlife Area north of Conconully is the oldest wildlife area in the state, set aside in 1939 to protect the winter range of mule deer.

LEFT

Beyond a grassy field of the Methow Wildlife Area, a thunderstorm hangs over the Cascade Mountains. The linear Methow Wildlife Area encompasses wildlife parcels east of the Methow River and along the valley foothills that together protect mule deer and blue grouse habitat.

At the annual Washington Outfitters and Guides Association's *Ride to Rendezvous*, it is easy to slip back in time. Have horse (or borrow one), will travel. Wagons, buckboards, and buggies round out the rendezvous train. Each May, some 100 adventurers make this five-day journey across the picturesque Methow Valley to the frontier village of Winthrop.

LEFT

The Winthrop Emporium is a town landmark. On the eastern front of the Cascades, the wooden sidewalks of Winthrop lead you into the Old West. The rustic, weathered-wood structures, old-fashioned business shields, and painted signs seal the town's late-1800s frontier spell. The town's founder, Guy Waring, opened the first general store here, supplying local ranchers and miners.

Winter's quiet spills over this orchard and barn in the Wenatchee River Valley in Chelan County. With the arrival of rail transportation and irrigation in the early 1900s, Chelan County rose to become an important producer of apples, cherries, peaches, plums, pears, and more recently, wine grapes.

LEFT

Plump pears hang from the tree at a Chelan County orchard.

Views across this orchard in bloom lead to beautiful Lake Chelan. Lake Chelan extends fifty-five miles into the heart of the Cascades. The lower lake is more arid, with irrigated orchards. The upper lake features fjordlike juts and stunning high peaks.

Yellow balsamroots cling to the summit of Chelan Butte and color the view to the Columbia River. Geologically one of the oldest mountains in the Pacific Northwest, Chelan Butte rises above the city of Chelan, extending grand views of the Lake Chelan Valley and the Columbia River drainage from its 3,800-foot summit. Here, at the top, reliable winds bend flowers but launch hang gliders.

Orchard Rock in Peshastin Pinnacles State Park puts an exclamation mark on this Wenatchee River Valley view. The state park's peculiar gallery of protruding rocks attracts rock climbers, hikers, and photographers. The rocks are Swauk sandstone.

ABOVE

Oak Creek Wildlife Area west of Naches along the Tieton and Naches Rivers is an important supplemental winter feeding station for elk and bighorn sheep, attracting, in turn, tourists. The nearly 95,000-acre wildlife area feeds about 1,200 elk, including many big bulls with full antler racks. January and February are the best months for elk viewing.

LEFT

The Cleman Mountain feeding station for the bighorn sheep at Oak Creek Wildlife Area can attract up to 150 bighorns at feeding time. The normally wild sheep pour out of the mountains as the feeding bins are filled. The native sheep disappeared in the 1930s; the Cleman Mountain herd of California bighorn was introduced in 1967. Historically, both California and Rocky Mountain bighorn sheep lived in Washington, and through reintroduction, they do again.

ABOVE

During the Ice Fest in January, fireworks light up the sky above the Leavenworth Gazebo and sledding hill. Always ready to celebrate, Leavenworth is a Bavarian-themed village tucked in a picturesque Cascade Mountains setting.

RIGHT

The players of the alpenhorns, the long signature horns of the Alps, pass during a Bavarian procession in Leavenworth. The town is so small that parades typically pass through the town twice. In the 1960s, when Leavenworth was spiraling downward after the departure of its rail and the failure of its mill, drastic action was needed. The town committed to reinventing itself as a "Little Bavaria," and the response was community-wide.

ABOVE

This Soul Salmon sculpture is on the conference center property of the Sleeping Lady Mountain Retreat in Leavenworth. The center emphasizes a strong commitment to art and nature in its meetings, so it was a natural placement for the art. The Soul Salmon project, a statewide public art project to raise awareness about the salmon, had a simple idea: Make the salmon visible through art.

RIGHT

Great Northern Railway memorabilia, including this ticket office, contribute to the offering at the Cashmere Pioneer Village and Museum, in Cashmere. The museum has an impressive Native American collection, with artifacts dating back 9,000 years, and its historic village brings together twenty original pioneer buildings from north-central Washington, including a mission, doctor's office, and school.

The sprawling Davidson Building holds a special place in the Ellensburg historic district and in town history. In 1889, when territorial citizens petitioned for statehood, Ellensburg hurried to build a state capital. But on July 4, 1889, fire struck the city and burned much of the downtown. Still seeking the capital, the town rallied and rebuilt. A phoenix on the Davidson Building symbolized the town's return from the ashes, but Ellensburg lost its bid for the capital.

Cherry blossom time is magical in Yakima County. Thanks to its nutrient-rich soil, warm temperatures, and irrigation water, Yakima County leads all counties in the nation in the production of apples, sweet cherries, winter pears, hops, and mint. The area has been dubbed "The Fruit Bowl of the Nation."

ABOVE

In the past decade, many Yakima County acres previously devoted to apples have been plowed under for grapes. Washington state rates second in the nation in wine production, and Yakima County accounts for much of that success.

The sweet cherry crop leads off fruit season in Yakima County. Over the past few years, the acreage in Washington devoted to cherries has increased, with recent crops setting records. Growers are adding later-ripening varieties, extending the cherry season into August.

This is no Red Delicious apple. The Red Delicious put Yakima County on the map, but today a single orchard may grow up to 100 varieties of Eve's tempting fruit. In 1980, the Red Delicious accounted for three-quarters of the Washington apple harvest. Now it represents about one-third of the state crop.

Lupines adorn Bird Creek Meadows on the southeastern base of Mount Adams, on the Yakama Indian Reservation. Threaded by sparkling streams, these meadows at the 6,000- to 6,500-foot elevation are acclaimed for their parade of wildflowers. The Yakama people consider Mount Adams sacred.

A bald eagle keeps watch on the Klickitat River from a snag perch. In 1963, bald eagle numbers had reached a dismal low of 417 documented pairs in the lower forty-eight states. This prompted the eagles' listing as an endangered species in forty-three states and as threatened in Washington, Oregon, Minnesota, Wisconsin, and Michigan. The recovery of the bald eagle, which is now on the fast track to a complete delisting, is a conservation success story.

This barn rests in the Klickitat Valley of Klickitat County. Barns are the working landmarks of rural Washington and the holders of history. Sadly, many barns across the nation are being torn down and replaced with modern storage buildings or housing developments.

The sun rises over a wintry Conboy Lake in Conboy Lake National Wildlife Refuge. In Klickitat County south of Mount Adams, this refuge encompasses 6,500 acres of the historic lakebed marsh that was drained for use by early settlers. The refuge provides habitat for 150 species of birds, deer, elk, beaver, and coyote.

ABOVE

On the Columbia River in Klickitat County, an Indian fishing platform sits below the John Day Dam, in a juxtaposed story of old and new. Historically, the tribes of the Columbia River fished the bountiful salmon runs, using dip nets from rustic wooden platforms, and the Klickitat people continue that tradition today. The dam harnessing the river represents power and modernization.

RIGHT

Rising out of the orchards, the Maryhill Community Church (1888) overlooks the Columbia River. This quaint little Victorian Christian chapel is on the National Register of Historic Places. The church was built to serve the community of Columbus, Washington, now long gone.

The Horse Heaven Hills provide this overlook of Prosser and the Yakima River and Valley. This rolling, hilly range stretches between Klickitat and Benton Counties. The rich grasses of the hills once supported wild horses.

A hot-air balloon floats past Horse Heaven Hills, during the Great Prosser Balloon Rally, held annually in Prosser. This is one of several hot-air balloon events that take to the skies of Washington. The Prosser rally attracts top fliers from around the Northwest.

The setting sun casts a golden glow on the White Bluffs at Hanford Reach National Monument. This lone national monument under the jurisdiction of the U.S. Fish and Wildlife Service protects the dry grass and bluff habitat along a rare free-flowing stretch of the Columbia River. Elsewhere along the river sit Hanford Reach's inactive plutonium reactors, historically linked to the "Fat Man" atomic bomb, dropped on Nagasaki, Japan, in August 1945, and to the Cold War.

On the Palouse River in the southeastern corner of the state, the thunderous torrent of Palouse Falls plunges 198 feet over a cliff in an awesome canyon amphitheater. Palouse Falls sits in the historic path of the Missoula Floods, which bulldozed much of the Northwest in a series of gargantuan floods stretched over a 2,000-year period, 17,000 years ago.

OPPOSITE

In Umatilla National Forest in Columbia County, Sheep Creek flows between green banks along the Tucannon River Trail. The unusual variety of flora along Sheep Creek prompted the U.S. Forest Service to designate the creek vicinity a Research Natural Area.

ABOVE

This longhorn swishes flies in the wide-open spaces of Asotin County, in the far southeastern corner of the state. Asotin County's earliest citizen, Robert Bracken, first engaged in cattle ranching here in 1861, back when it was Indian country. Agriculture continues to be a mainstay of the economy.

In Asotin County, the furrowed, dry conifer slopes of Asotin Wildlife Area meet in a "V" at Asotin Creek. This wildlife area is a major elk calving and wintering range and serves mule deer, bighorn sheep (introduced here), bears, cougars, and other animal and bird species.

Within Nez Perce National Historical Park, two rock outcroppings compose the Buffalo Eddy Petroglyphs, one on each side of the Snake River. This decorated rock sits in Washington, south of Asotin; the other outcropping is across the river in Idaho. The art dates back 4,500 years to the early Nez Perce people.

These silhouettes at Granite Lake Park in Clarkston, Washington, commemorate the Lewis and Clark Expedition (1803–1806). The figures of William Clark, Meriwether Lewis, and Sacajawea overlook an impound on the Snake River to the dry canyon slope.

In Walla Walla County, this railroad track along the Columbia River at Wallula Gap disappears to the horizon. Wallula Gap is a mile-wide opening in the basalt anticlines (folds) of the Columbia River Basin. When the deluging waters of the historic Missoula Floods reached this bottleneck, the waters backed up the Snake River to the Salmon River, forming temporary Lake Lewis.

The rolling agricultural region known as the Palouse stretches across the southeastern corner of Washington, south of Spokane, and across the Moscow area of Idaho. In mid-June, the green wheat-fields interspersed with fields of canola, dry peas, and lentils paint an artful landscape dotted by barns and traced by rural roads. This overview is from Steptoe Butte in Steptoe Butte State Park, north of Colfax, Washington.

Did someone say stop? This stop-action shot came during the Colfax Junior Rodeo in Colfax. Summer is rodeo season, with professional, amateur, and junior competitions bringing riders into arenas across the state.

A feathered fan cools this Treaty Day Princess as she rides on a parade float during the Yakama Nation Treaty Day Commemoration in Toppenish. The Treaty of 1855 established the Yakama Indian Reservation, giving the Yakama people a permanent homeland. It also secured tribal hunting and fishing rights. Similar treaties were struck with other Northwest tribes that same year.

BELOW

The annual Spokane Tribal Labor Day Powwow on the Spokane Indian Reservation in Wellpinit attracts native peoples from throughout the Northwest. During the young males dance competition, dancers bounce, spin, and swirl about the tribal judge, their feathers, beads, and colored regalia becoming a rainbow blur.

The present Monroe Street Bridge in downtown Spokane faithfully recreated the singular qualities of the old 1911 Monroe Street span, a sentimental city landmark noted for its high concrete-arch construction and ornamental detail. The modern bridge's improved pedestrian walkway also offers superb views of the Spokane River Falls.

At Spokane's Manito Park, Duncan Garden captivates with its symmetry, colorful plant choices, granite fountain, and evergreen background. It was designed and built by John W. Duncan in 1913 and demonstrates a European Renaissance style. Manito Park, a premier public park, has served the Spokane community for more than 100 years. Its name means "Spirit of Nature."

LEFT

The Riverfront Park Pavilion is a landmark of the "Lilac City." In 1974, Spokane hosted the World's Fair alongside the Spokane River, and the 100-acre Riverfront Park is a legacy of that time. This steel-cable structure from the United States World Fair pavilion now holds the amusement park and ice skating rink.

LEFT

The Colfax Codger Pole is one-of-a-kind art. This sixty-five-foot carved wooden pole wears the mature faces of the 1938 Colfax High football team. Colfax lost to rival St. John at the original game, but won the rematch fifty years later when all players were in their sixties. The game caught national attention, and this chainsaw sculpture by Jonathan LaBenne preserves "Codger Bowl" history for posterity.

Quiet moments are easy to come by in lightly populated Pend Oreille County at the northeastern corner of the state. At the Canadian border, this county is wild enough for moose, caribou, bighorn sheep, mountain goats, and even grizzly bears. On the county's fifty-five lakes, you can hear the sound of the loon or witness the flight of an eagle.

As the shadows lengthen, the fly-line of a solitary fisherman dances over the surface of Long Lake in Colville National Forest. At the northeastern corner of the state, Colville National Forest encompasses the forest lands around the Kettle River Range and Selkirk Mountains. These rounded mountains geologically are akin to the Rocky Mountains.

LEFT

This ponderosa pine cone is at Lake Roosevelt National Recreation Area. The ponderosa pine dominates the dry forest slopes of eastern Washington. Named for its ponderous size and weighty wood, the pine was first described by botanist explorer David Douglas, from specimens collected in eastern Washington, during his 1825 to 1827 North American travels.

In Lake Roosevelt National Recreation Area, this open ponderosa pine stand is on Mission Point. Lake Roosevelt, the 130-mile-long impound on the upper Columbia River formed by the Depression-era construction of Grand Coulee Dam under President Franklin D. Roosevelt's WPA program, provides wet outdoor recreation in the arid northeast corner of the state.

The Old Molson Ghost Town Museum, in Molson, near the Canadian border in the north-central part of the state, preserves frontier history. The reassembled pioneer town consists of authentic buildings, artifacts, and historic equipment. Seen here are the law office and Old Shingle Mill.

The sculpture *Grandfather Cuts Loose the Ponies* complements the sunrise above the Columbia River in Grant County. The life-size metal silhouettes, by sculptor David Govedare, depict the Native American legend of the Great Spirit's gift of horses to humans.

About the Authors

George and Rhonda Ostertag have been exploring Washington and the Pacific Northwest for more than twenty years, uncovering the region's prized haunts and raptures. As a professional nature and travel photographer, George has worked independently and in collaboration with his author-wife, Rhonda, to produce numerous books and articles. Ostertag's photography commonly appears in calendars and on postcards. George and Rhonda most recently collaborated on Voyageur Press' *Our Oregon* and *Backroads of Oregon*.